Balancing
on a barbed wire fence

Jack Withers

Argyll
publishing

First published in 1995 by
Argyll Publishing
Glendaruel
Argyll PA22 3AE

Acknowledgements are due to Chris Bruder, Nürnberg for her kind
permission to use the picture *Isolation* on the cover; to Gordon Meade
for using *The Cage*; Scottish Child who first published *Pram Time*; Open
World and Radical Scotland where other work first appeared in whole
or in part.
The publisher wishes to acknowledge the kind support of Letterewe
Estate towards the cost of publishing this book.

British Library Cataloguing-in-Publication Data.
**A catalogue record for this book is available from the British
Library.**

ISBN 1 874640 76 9

Origination
Cordfall, Glasgow, G4 9RH

Printing
Cromwell Press, Wiltshire SN12 8PH

To Bea,

and to those who know me,
to those who care

"If our work as writers cannot be understood as criticism, as opposition and resistance, as an awkward question, as a challenge to power, then we write in vain . . . we (only) decorate the slaughterhouse with geraniums."

Günter Eich

Contents

Preface

Jack Withers was born in pre-World War Two Glasgow
into what was then considered to be an ordinary family
living in public housing. His family were like all those
around them in their efforts to keep body and soul together
through work, subject to the vagaries of the free market.
Like most of his peers he left school at the earliest
opportunity and joined the search for a job. Years, and
many gainful, and some painful, positions later, he took up
writing. He writes about what he experiences in the world.

In this sense, Jack Withers is no different from anybody
who writes — making marks on paper about what they
experience. But in another, more important and much
more absorbing way, Jack Withers' writing is entirely
individual and unique. Like all writers who are directed by
conscience, his work is the very essence of human
individuality, the true antidote to tyranny, pomposity and
inflated power in any form.

Take the very term 'poet' to start with. Anyone who has
heard Jack Withers perform at a poetry reading will know
that he is more likely to burst into song than read piously
from a prepared page. He appears not to need any prepared
script, reciting as if from memory. And when you listen to
the sense of the words, you realise they probably come from
a good deal deeper down than mere memory. He eschews
the preciousness that the word 'poetry' generates in certain

circles. He is never more delighted when people in pubs after readings, spontaneously enthuse — "I never realised poetry was like this, anything to do with anything in *my* life."

It is these feelings of being disconnected from each other's experience of living in the modern world that is a constant preoccupation. While the very essence of human life lies in our capacity to share — common language, knowledge, fate — Jack Withers is scathing of the antisocial forces that fragment and distance us from each other. Life becomes all the poorer for the destruction of what binds us together and keeps us sane.

So poetry should be full of life and not be like other fragmented bits of reality cut off from the rest. Unusually for a poetry collection, this one contains work by another poet, Gordon Meade. His *The Cage* was inspired by a shared experience. By responding, Jack Withers points away from the concept of the lonely poet, introspective and alone with his art.

So the reader will not be surprised by the themes in this collection of work from the last ten years. Balancing on a barbed wire fence may well be an apt metaphor for the human condition as experienced by the majority of us. Contemplating the state of humanity, as Withers does in the title piece, from the peaceful, bright, breathtaking, snow-covered heights of Ben Wyvis or Ben Lawers only contrasts the more with the state of affairs in the city below.

In a society ever more divided, life down there is not, after all, anything at all like a sylvan grove. Withers' city may be Glasgow, his country Scotland, but the truths he writes prevail as universals. Relationships between individuals who consider themselves as not belonging, who feel themselves to be strangers in their own land are observed in all their harshness. Those in the privileged third of western societies literally do not know the half of it. The unemployed and dispossessed added to the proportion of those in lowly rewarded or insecure employment make up the majority not just on the streets that Jack Withers walks.

So whether mothers, lovers, partners or public officials, fellow citizens can relate according to values of callous inhumanity. We develop defences to the horror of the consequences. The role of the writer, if that is worth anything, is to expose and examine the truths in the world we have created. In many of the pieces in this collection, Jack Withers creates his art around this sometimes difficult task.

An item on the radio, an overheard snippet in the bus queue or in the fish shop is enough to set the writer his work. One of Withers' most moving and I think awesomely beautiful pieces, *Past Caring*, published in his *A Real Glasgow Archipelago* collection, was inspired by the murder of a Glasgow prostitute by her husband. In the frustration and anger of domestic violence, there are no winners. In the savage acting out of revenge on a mugger in *Encounter*, published here for the first time, no-one comes out with head high.

Scotland, that marginal enigma of a nation, does not escape without dissection. During a protracted correspondence, initiated by the poet Alan Bold in the pages of *The Scotsman* newspaper in the early 1980s, Withers wrote two tongue-in-cheek suggestions for an alternative national anthem — *Bold thoughts on two anthems*. His *Mock Up* and *A Hearty Scottish Welcome to* don't miss the target of Scots cringing and spineless readiness to 'sell their granny' either.

Jack Withers is by no means confined to local concerns.

BALANCING

His piece *Six Days that Shook you up* written on return from
a visit to Rostov in 1991 raises international items as
diverse as toilet facilities as a measure of national psyche
to superpower posturing. Living as he does in a part of
Scotland which contains the highest concentration of
civilian and military nuclear activity in the whole of
western Europe, he is sharp in *No Ant is Trident*. His *Scottish
Writers Against the Bomb*, reading from just ten years ago
now as if from a time past, is acute on the role of the writer
in passing comment on the important items that are
conveniently abandoned by party machines in pursuit of
higher power.

    Reading Jack Withers will inspire a sense of value and
urgency to uphold respect for fellow men and women.
Bursting into song may not be everyone's idea of literature,
but Withers work is about far far more than merely
decorating the house.

Derek Rodger
Publisher
September 1995

Balancing on a barbed wire fence

Let's halt a minute.
Only a minute?
It's so silent, so quiet.
Quite. Like being so close to a glimpse of the ultimate.
Like being at the centre of the universe. Intense.
Immense.
I can hardly believe it.
Believe what?
That we're so close to the summit.
Another hundred feet and that'll be that. Pinnacle of light.
Way out?
I'm amazed at how we're still so fit.
Regular exercise and strict diet erects a barrier against the
steady rot.
What an incredible sky. Deep blue eye of infinity. Makes
you ask why.
O to be an angel and able to fly.
Wi wings o' fine feathers.
Soaring over Wyvis and Lawers.
I can't believe in angels.
Only in avenging vandals?
City horrors.
Nature's mirrors?
What a glorious day.

BALANCING

High and still dry above distant Loch Tay. Ecstasy.
Nevertheless that's quite a stiff breeze.
We'll have it behind us when we descend on the skis.
Snow, snow, wonderful snow. Two isolated dots on a vast
plateau.
It's so difficult to decide on a favourite view, over to Ben
More and Venue or across at Nevis frae Bidean in Glencoe.
Or the islands o' Loch Lomond frae high on Ben Lomond.
Or the Isle o' Mull frae Pulpit Hill.
Bonnie Scotland whaur dae ye stand?
It really makes you wonder why people still hate and maim
and kill.
Some hot sweet tea?
Insanity. Gadarene swine unable to see.
Let's enjoy it while we're still free.
Are we? or do we balance on a barbed wire fence?
I feel like an insect suspended in space.
Chronic sickness o' the human race.
Would you risk it for a biscuit?
And as for the proletariat.
Forget it.
Forget it?
Aye.
Only when I keel over and die.
We're here for enjoyment.
But there's no escaping the human predicament.
What's that peak way over there on the skyline?
Stobinian. Ben A' An am Binnein. What a breathtaking and
stunning horizon.
My opinion is let's enjoy ourselves while we still can.
Self-indulgence?
Common sense.
Not so common.

Likewise with acute and heightened existence.
It's all about balance and intelligence while still remaining
human.
If you can, you mean.
I can no longer see the Ben and I'm shivering. Let's start
climbing again.
Up and away into the dying day. Zip-up. Flask away. Skis
on.
Air like wine. Sky, space and old man mountain.
And here again comes that hot spring sun.
Who can explain emotion?
Or the joy and liberating sensation that comes from sheer
effort, sweat and elegant motion?
It's almost unbearable.
Trying in vain to postpone what is surely inevitable?

Lanarkshire Miner

a very strong man
was Sam Trueman

they called him
the Iron Man
of the Priory Pit

when they were in a jam
down in the pit
they'd send for Sam
and he'd get them out of it

once a cable
had snapped
on the lift-shaft cage
but Sam survived
the fall
to see again
King Billy on his white horse
up on the living-room wall

yes
a straight man
was

Sam Trueman
no one
in entire
Blantyre
ever able once
to call him a liar

he was a hard worker
and a collier
a true
Lanarkshire miner
and man

Scottish writers against the bomb

(first published in *Radical Scotland* August 1984)

There were times when the writer felt he was getting precisely nowhere. Oh yes, a few of his "nuclear predicament" stories had been published in small magazines but the reaction to them had been minimal. Not a mention from a critic or even a friend. One guy he knew though, had said: "Your story wasn't bad," grinned and moved on rapidly before he could even ask him why it "wasn't bad".

People often terrified the writer just as much as the nuclear predicament did. In fact, in one of his stories he'd tried to show that if only the human predicament could somehow be solved then, of course, there would be no nuclear, ecological, or demographic predicaments worth speaking of. An ideal world and yet another illusion of fatalism was the norm everywhere. Even in the ranks of the nuclear activists so few seemed to have the sense of horror and extreme urgency within them that the writer had. "Don't make trouble" he'd once been told on a picnic of a demonstration as the police might react.

Trouble? Trouble? God!
Yes, this was the seemingly insoluble problem: the realisation that the time for playing games with higher authority was now over. However, these truths did not

weaken the writer's resolve to continue with the task he
had set himself, trying to explore imaginatively the complex
issues of the imminent holocaust through the medium of
the written word. For what else was he to do? Do a
somersault and aim to become a big-time writer of sugary
romances or spy-stories?
Existence would be unbearable if he were to throw his
hand in now. Somehow he must continue with his mission
to alert and teach. Somehow. Again he thought of going
full time, but no, he couldn't, his part-time job as art
teacher keeping him in touch with life in the raw, and of
course keeping the wolf from the door also. And besides, he
was concerned at the moment with his frequent moods of
black despair and nightmarish sleeps which he attributed to
his determined writings. The thought of an increase in the
same terrified him. No, he had to live with himself, isolated
as he felt he was from most. There was no other alternative.
Time was precious.

And so he continued with his creative obsession, even more
resolved than before to discover the truth of the matter
through the exhaustive concentration of the artistic trance.
Through the revelations of his own psyche and
temperament, he would somehow succeed, that he was
convinced of. Or was he? Constantly assailed as he was by
insecurity and an occasional bout of self-doubt, the writer
understandably had to often convince himself to be
convinced of something. He knew, as well as I do, that this
was the only antidote to constant throughts of suicide or
insanity. Booze and drugs were not. Booze and drugs were
killers. He was trying to prevent death, not induce it; and
he was seeking clarity, not confusion.
The possibilities inherent in the holocaust were infinite, he

had discovered. Initially, he had suspected that a couple of
stories and a poem or two would bleed the vein dry, but he
was proved wrong. Once the imagination got going, all
sorts of variations presented themselves like growths in a
swamp, a fertile swamp. The writer considered that he had
succeeded with a few of these growths but failed with most.
He wondered if he should try and rework some of the
growths he'd failed with or try and develop new ones. Until
now he had refrained from using real names of countries,
governments, presidents, missiles and so on, preferring to
rely upon metaphor and allegory and imaginary futuristic
holocausts, to try and get at the essence of it all. This may
have been a mistake, he judged, as the reality of the
situation itself is so terrifyingly real. Perhaps then, he would
be better employed concentrating on the real facts; facts like
the complex mentalities of the two nuclear giants, the USA
and the USSR for instance; like individuals, no country can
escape from its own historical experience, a fact that the
writer understood only too well, being Scottish. And then
there was Vietnam, Germany, Poland, Ireland and Israel,
perfect examples; all schizophrenic patients trapped in
asylums of the past, and unable to scale the high security
walls to relative freedom. No, memories can't be scrubbed
clean like sinks.

Opposite polarities of fear: the USSR, with their memories
of twenty million dead resulting from invasion and
occupation of their land by fascistic forces, and the USA
living neurotically with the psychosis of what it might be
like to have at one strike, in a sudden flash, sixty of seventy
million dead throughout their country. The red native
Americans with their memories of invasion and genocide
are another matter entirely of course, and who would blame

them if they saw it all as being a deserved retribution of justice for the hordes of greedy rapacious killers who had descended on them from the east.

Histories of horror creating an abnormal world by an abnormal species. It all went wrong somehow. The abilities of the gifted few to discern and create beauty out of the struggle for existence and to show a possible way forward, is always suppressed by the inadequate psychopaths who inevitably rise to real power. Nero, Napoleon, Nixon, Ubico, Hitler, Duvalier; or Socrates, Christ, St Francis of Assisi, Michelangelo, Mozart, Mandelstam — Jeckyll and Hydes of humanity, who should we learn from? Isn't it obvious? No, it doesn't seem to be, otherwise we wouldn't be in the morass that we're in. We are weighed down by mass conformity to the wrong structures and goals that we have been manipulated into accepting. We've lost our roots, the natural balances and checks of so-called primitive nature. We are destroying it as well as ourselves. Compelled education is a contradiction. The wild and uneducated dingo will kill some of its young when necessary; we don't, we are educated, and will continue to pollute the world until it is too late.

The mediocre have inherited the earth, the not so meek mediocre, controllers of governments, committees and institutions, who will inevitably silence any solitary voice of sanity by any measure available to them. Even if the truth may occasionally be glimpsed beyond the confines of the tunnel, it will be ignored in the cause of conformity. Silence the rebels, at all cost. Plod on. Blinkered.

To the writer, these were the simple truths of a complex

world. He at least was clear about them, much more so than I was in fact. Full of self-doubts, and not on the same level of understanding as the writer, I found it very difficult indeed to see my way through the traumas of existence here on earth. There was so much confusion and in any case life is far too short and ephemeral for any sense ever to be made out of it. It was no wonder that people soon gave up the struggle for some kind of comprehension and simply accepted all that was dished out to them from governments, tyrants, con-men and the mass-media. They allowed themselves to be conditioned, but then, like the writer, I saw that this was where the trouble stemmed from.

I haven't given up the struggle as yet. I couldn't live with myself if I did, there being too much horror in the world for that. The writer, and many other similar writers and artists, people of vision and love, are helping me to pursue comprehension. Those who are and have been concerned, that is; those with resolve and insight. The committed. Those are my leaders and guides. I need help, they need help, we all need help. We have such energy and potential, but for what? Busyness and business are not enough; we must work hard at exploring the mystery of existence otherwise it is meaningless; look out into space and into ourselves. Concentration. Intensity. Discipline. Don't escape from the herd; stay with it, change it, yourself along with it.

Our Father

Like some alien visitor from another star
our father returned from the war far wiser
than he'd ever been in his life before
at least that's what he said and that he'd
been very lucky indeed not to have been one of the many dead
who'd spilled their blood in pursuit of the great crusade

But o how sad it was then to watch him pick his
way about with that pathetic white stick horrific it was
as it made us feel sick and so nervous and helpless
that is until he got us all to swear from his chair
to struggle like hell for peace and to outlaw war
as he felt deep in his bones that the next one was near
and then each one of us would of course become a cool killer
as it's so easy to learn how to murder and slaughter

Rapidly thereafter he went down the slippery hill
and that was that another sad funeral where the church bell
nearby seemed to toll out that it's criminal to kill
he'd taught us how to think and how to feel farewell
farewell we'll remember him well
and how he convinced us all that war was hell

Hammer So Fickle

A worker is using a hammer. He cuts quite a figure.
Chips of stone are flying everywhere, I the spectator.
The stunning sound I can no longer ignore as isolated
creator, thus I try to work it into the general picture.
So, should we need a reminder, Christ was a carpenter,
who in his robe fashioned a way-out wardrobe with saw,
plane, nails and screwdriver. There it stood in its cosmic
corner and never went anywhere other than to be witness
to Jehovah as he bent over working, wandering and
suffering.
Unvarnished and untarnished it shall remain for ever and
ever as a puzzle to all men. Amen. But continue to probe.

Deid Regular

As if frae a no sae distant skinklin staur ice–cauld
frae afar I tak tent o this timeless saison o hale
and guid cheer a heichmaist pynt o the year so we
hear as yet again it's here

fowk greet and lauch whyles unnerneath they saftly
breathe in fumes of flouers and lang-lost oors as
sclimmin blinds ower memory's minds shaws a glisk o
staurlit lift ayont for the myth is noo rale and wi'
wellin luve they feel for each the ither when baubles
and babies they see ablow yirdly tree gowd a' upon it
like lichts o infinity

and frae athort unkent space mony a ticht face
freezes and listens spierin the thrab o blin eternity
and carvin a curve o muckle warmth and luve mulled
frae the past that noo has come tae pass but wull
agin be lost en masse but at lang last the greatest
thocht o a' had come though only tae some and e'en
tae the dumb wha kens wha'll be crucified the nicht

oan some brutal hill and in the dyin licht

City Garden

City garden
Quite close to the Kelvin
And fellow gardeners Knox and Calvin

Where the air seems so sweet
In spite of the heat

With special smell

And a squirrel
Yes a squirrel dances along the wall
With perfect curl to its tail

Does it know
This is Glasgow?

This veritable garden of eden
Where creepers trail
And bees buzz off heavily laden
As worms create their own little hell

Then the squirrel shoots up the old lime tree
The thorn below in its bower so green
As berries blacken under a big hot sun
And a thrush celebrates all that's free

Where moggies hide from maurauding doggies
Where swallows chase insect shadows
And roses and daisies pose

Chattering starling
Robin and wren
Hunting and killing
Death in the sun

Blackbirds stab again and again
Messing up the fresh mown lawn

Sudden murder
Of scuttling spider

I shudder
And think of famine
And hear elsewhere

The earth crying out for rain.

Pram Time

I waken and hear talking.
Something inside is almost breaking.

Shadows are still dancing and walking.
I'm all alarm and stink like a farm.
But . . . I am, I am, I still am.

I assume it is the same old room.
Yes. And then in my milky dwam
I hear a distant voice utter the sound . . . pram.

I keep mum
Listening to the run and trickle of an inner stream.

Warm home, warm home, warm home.

Then like a beating drum
Or recurrent dream
I abruptly give vent to a pent-up scream.
But in a vacuum.
Come, come, come,
Someone. Come.

Full of drooling spittle,

Knowing so little
In this constant battle
For what they call my bottle.

No wonder I bite on my thumb
And dream of the womb.
Faces appear which slobber and coo.
Most false, so few true.

Who are you, who are you, who are you?

Everything's new
And I seem to swim, to swim, to swim.

I fear the light,
I fear the dark.
I wake at night
And hear them talk.

Panic.
Sick.

Someone come, someone come, someone come.

Under attack,
They call it home, home, home.

Dad . . . light . . . cat . . . tit . . . mum,
My name . . . I am, I am, I still . . . am.

More of the Same Only Different

A message boy I am
And a message boy
I'll remain
And the message I bring
to everyone
Is that I'm not alone
in being insane

        Beaten as a child
        because he was wild
        Little boy black & blue

        Now he's old
        And still out in the cold
        Struggling to continue

        He lives in a prison
        His anger is frozen
        Nothing any more is new

        He is all male
        And learned to kill
        How easily it could have been you

Haw Maw

Maw got anither maggot inside the cot
An no long efter that
She saw that we'd caught anither rat.
She thought it hud shot
Its bolt but it hudnae.
Whit a fright she got
And she shot straight intae the cludgie.

We hammered oan the door
An shoutit intae her
"Haw Maw, haw Maw, ur ye a'right Maw?"
Feelin jist as anxious as yon
Ither time
When she was oan the lager-and-lime
An she wis weepin an screamin
An threatenin tae shoot the craw.

But efter a bit
We heard her say that it wis OK
That she'd been badly bit
But that she'd be oot in a minute;
An sure as shit she wis back oot
Askin whit a' the fuss wis aboot,
An that it wis jist anither bite

BALANCING

Frae a hauf-deid rat.
Then she said it could've been a lot worse,
A mugger rapin an muggin her
An stealin her purse
Or sumthin.
But this, this is nuthin, she said, suckin
Her finger,
For think o' a' yon hunger elsewhere
Oot there in Africa an Asia
A' yon terrible scenes ye see oan the telly.
That's real worry.
Yon wid make ye stick yir heid in the oven.
Thank Christ thir's nae population explosion
In Govan.
Or famine.
Thank Christ. But noo ah need a rest. An she
Took wan as she liked tae look her best.
Some wumman oor Maw.

Some wumman.

Love File

Starved of exciting intimate relationships?
Attractive single sport-loving professional male, late 40s,
ex-weight-lifter, recent divorcee, is desperate to find that
special someone to fill that huge gaping hole in his boring
everyday existence. Loves walking, talking, eating,
laughing,
sleeping, boomerang-throwing, day-dreaming and dancing.
Own
flat, car, gun, garden, dish-washer and washing-machine.
Phone and have fun.
Voice Link Number 4567 – dial quick, darling, and you'll
soon find yourself in heaven.

Are you lonesome out there?
Voluptuous vivacious divorcee in her 30s and of Gipsy
origin, is into cinema, ballroom-dancing, especially tango
and rumba, awaits a cute Cupid to come up and shaft her
some time.
Hobbies: eating-out, hang-gliding, ski-ing and occasional
pub-crawling. Loves to feel those goose-pimples moving
dramatically. Lives for the week-ends. So, guys, how's
about being prepared to lose yourself in one super pair of
big brown eyes? You don't know what you're missing –
yet.
Voice Link Number 1212 – bring some booze and drink
from my shoe.

Urgent Visit

Hmm, now let me see
Said my very busy GP
You say you've got this
Eternally recurrent dream
About World War Three
During which you wake up abruptly
Dying for a pee

That's correct, I said
Night after night
And it's as if the whole world
Is consumed
In a great blinding light

Hmm, you've got it bad
Real bad indeed, he said
But actually there's very little
To be said as it's all
Bound up with your own disturbed head
And not with the real world outside
With its living and its dead

Aye, where millions get killed
And there's horrors untold

I should have said
To the smooth bourgeois bastard
But I didn't – coward
Instead I asked
But what then about me
And my dying for a pee
Hasn't it got something to do
With my screwed-up head?

Hmm, he said, don't be absurd
For that also is in the mind
And now if you don't mind
Me being cruel to be kind
Your symptoms and disease
If disease is what it is
Is endemic to the whole of mankind

And yes, that was that
My unnecessary visit
Had come to an end

Encounter

That anonymity of early morning in the city. Outlook black
There had been pressure before when you felt as if you
were going to crack.
It must have been around 2 o'clock. Confrontation. Sudden
shock.

"Right Jimmy. Money. The lot. Give. And quick. OK?"

You felt real sick and you felt yourself tighten, shudder and
shake.

Your first impulse was to turn and run but when he
produced a gun –
Dummy one or not – you didn't and you couldn't. Not
when you're faced
With something so frightening, barbaric and ignorant. What
a predicament.
Right in the shit, they call it.

OK, you say, gesturing, wait a minute, and you stuck your
hand into your
Anorak-pocket just as if you were going for your wallet. It
was a real
Pregnant moment as you'd almost forgotten that unknown

to your wee wife
You carried a knife to protect your life.

Then, blood coursing up into your brain, like a madman
you went for the cunt
Stabbing and ripping with manic delight into the bastard's
fat gut as
You heard him gasp, gag and moan, then issue a wet and
skittery huge fart.
And you too so humane and intelligent.

Like going through the motions. Like a dream. Everything
somehow so distant.

But then through a red mist you withdrew the knife with a
sickening twist
And like a lump of meat the bastard fell back against the
graffitied wall.

Who was now the criminal you heard yourself yell. Who is
fucking ill?
You who'd always fought for the downtrodden lumpen
proletariat.
You can hardly believe it.

Some sleeping giant. More like an ignorant ant. Thank
Christ it was dark.
Sick. Distressed. Paranoiac. You got off your mark over the
fence and
Down through the silent park. Self-defence the best
method of attack?

Thoughts and emotions uneven you chuck the fucking
weapon into the Kelvin.

BALANCING

Home again. No one is in. You search for any
incriminating sin. None.
You open a can, turn on the television and switch off the
phone. No dream.
It's real. A not so cool kill. Imminent that silent scream.
Soul in hell.
And prison will be no heaven.

The Cage

by Gordon Meade for Jack Withers

Last night, I hear tell of a cage,
Perched on a hill, made to catch crows.

Baited with a sheep's carcase,
It's sides slanted down towards

An inviting gap that trapped unwary
Scavengers. Lured by the stench of

Rotten flesh, all they could do was
wait until the farmer came with a .22.

Shot up through the head, the crows
Would be hung upside-down, on

A barbed-wire fence, or nailed
By their wings to the farm's barn-

Door as a warning to others - NO LAMB
STEALERS TOLERATED ON THESE COLD MOORS

A horrendous tale, a horror story.
But more horrendous, the workings

Of the mind that spawned the thought,
The body that sprouted the feet that

Walked towards the spot, the hands
That made the cage, and the fingers

That pulled the trigger that fired
The shot. Tremendous, the blackness

Of crows, so natural. Terrific,
The whiteness of sheep, so abused.
Horrendous and horrific,
the greyness of man.

The Cage

Gordon Meade's poem *The Cage* was to me a revelation and
made me wonder if any other parallels exist of one poet
creating a poem out of another poet's "telling of the story".
Co-productions, merging of the imaginations, so to speak.
Intriguing.

It all happened during a geopoetic week-end at Allershaw
in Lanarkshire in the late Autumn. Bea and I were first to
arive at the lonely Chekhovian mansion late on a gey dreich
Friday afternoon in the autumn. A couple of hours of
daylight remained so we set out for a wee dawdle up the
hill to give us an appetite, and it was up there just off a road
that seemed to lead up and over to nowhere that we saw
the cage. What the hell's that strange construction up there,
I said, pointing. Something from outer space or a Max Ernst
symbol brought to life? Up we went, cagily, and there it
was, dead sinister: more evidence of man's ingenuity and
cruelty when dealing with other forms of (low) life,
especially "pests". The caged crow flapped around in alarm
ignoring the half-eaten sheep's carcase and no doubt sensing
that its mortal enemy, man, had arrived to exterminate it.
Nice little touch, too: whoever had constructed the cage
had provided a wooden perch for the crow to sit on and
take a rest between bouts of frantic flapping about searching
for a way out. As "townies" but lovers of the countryside
we shuddered with horror and wondered if only crows
were pulled in or were other winged pests also trapped now
and again. Bea wanted to open the bolted and heavily-
bound with wire door but I said better not as maybe
someone had a Kalashnikov rifle trained on us. And then
you never know, I added, maybe it's not a trap for pests at

all; for all we know it could be some kind of advanced scientific experiment to test the fear-threshold of the crow family. Something vitally important, perhaps not in the same league as, say, our protective Trident missiles, but important nevertheless. Still, they might have used rats instead of nice crows.

The following day we went up to the cage again and the crow was still there going through the motions. What were its thoughts, we wondered. But then crows don't have thoughts unlike man the superior species. Poor things. When will they ever learn?

Stranger

Such a strange one he was
Always at a distance from us all:
But there was no escape-clause,
We all knew the drill.

Whenever he spoke
The sense was intensely black;
Implying that one must go for broke
Or else they'll hammer you back.

He said he looked inside his head
To grapple with the demon within,
Where a hidden sun can give a sign
That one can learn from the dead.

To love thy neighbour or murder her,
To knock on each bolted door;
To walk through streets of horror,
Menace from along the corridor.

Here where man hides from the sun
And picks the locks of cellars,
It's continuous abuse and use of gun
By hired gorillas and cool killers.

He knew not what he came to teach
In dance, in street or in trance;
As a place of peace was out of reach
For all who killed off conscience.

All that is technical is unnatural,
They've silenced the green machine;
Not elemental but artificial
Is the reaction of men unclean.

Scared

Scared at what's inside your head
Scared at times to go to bed
Scared of when yon whistle will blow
Scared to find there's nowhere to go

Scared to watch the nine o'clock news
Scared by always singing the blues

Scared of the love that once used to be
Scared of the thought of creeping insanity

Scared of all those unable to think and feel
Scared of a world without any ideal
Scared of existence and its terrifying enigma
Scared of failing to reach Utopia

Scared of wars
Scared of the stars
Scared of motorways jammed with cars

Scared of monotonous and endless tomorrows
Scared of those sick creations by William Burroughs

Scared of those zombies who can torture others

Scared of ambitious fathers and mothers
Scared by fellow-travellers in packed aerodromes
Scared by the resonances of the deepest poems

Scared by that yellow moon in a black-hole sky
Scared by knowing you're soon going to die

Scared by cities
Scared by authorities
Scared by mankind's continuous atrocities

Scared of the wail of a warning siren
Scared by the numbers seven and thirteen

Scared of never getting a foothold in an alien world
Scared by all that makes your blood run cold

Scared of pills
Scared of high walls
Scared of mankind's insoluble ills

Scared of those creatures who whisper through the night
Scared by your own spiritual plight

Scared by neighbours who don't want to know you
Scared by relationships without any value

Scared of repetition
Scared of destruction
Scared of never arriving at an end-solution

As to why you're so scared

Bold thoughts on two anthems

16 Belmont Crescent, Glasgow,
August 10, 1983
Sir, The shire is really in dire straights these days. Me too.
But up from the depths of my extreme nausea at the futility
of it all welled the following two anthem/laments that I
envisage being sung by either Andy Stewart or Tammy
Troot to inspire the massed patriots of Scotshire as we get
tore intae thae Sassenachs at Hampden Park or Murrayfield.
Bold thoughts? Yes, perhaps, but someone has to be or else
we may end up losing our regional identity altogether in
the near future if we're not careful. Shame.

Bloom O' Dignity
(Tune: Hey, Tuttie Taitie)
Demonstrate and agitate
For unemployment's no our fate
We'll fight oan an aggravate
The worker's enemy (oorsels?)

Con-men an entrepreneurs
Capital an profiteers
Iscariots an saboteurs
Scabs o' liberty

We must be forged wi' fire an steel
Tae crush for guid the exploiter's heel
An win the right for a commonweal
O' honest equality

The past is there for a' tae see
Blood-soaked times o' slavery
So we must learn frae history
Tae banish misery

But cloods are there as daurk as night
Blackin oot yon precious light
An we'll a' dee if we don't unite
In solidarity

So when's the day an when's the hour
When we tak up the reigns o' power
Tae cultivate prood freedom's flooer
Bloom o' dignity

Bonnie Scotland
(Tune: Red River Valley)

Thir's a country they ca' bonnie Scotland
It's a place that we don't know that well
Cause it's owned by the big multinationals
And them who only live tae buy an sell

Well if ye think o' yon fitba' battalions
An the millions who never say boo
It's nae wunner the factories ur closing
An plenty feenish up oan the burroo

BALANCING

O' ye'll see the Scots trottin doon tae London
When yet anither twenty thoosan jine the dole
Cause they dinna want tae rule their ain dominion
An dae awa' for guid wi' the beggin bowl

So if thir's a future for Scotland
An it's airmies o' dinna bother me
Scots must fight against yon monsters ca'd Trident
Or it's cheerio tae life an liberty.

Hearty Scottish Welcome To

all foreign capital for this is bonnie scotland –
not ulster oh no and most certainly not england –

so peaceful sleepy-eyed and calm
and giving no cause for any untoward alarm
or that you could come to trouble or harm

mark you there's still the odd wee strike or two
instigated by those trots and commies luckily only a few
who mostly are now safely on the burroo
and as for all those hoary myths about the red clyde
forget it as it's such a much more sensible generation now
so nicely manipulated and doped and cowed

little danger of that lot again taking up the role of patriot
being much more like robots now than the true proletariat
the big boot of course now being on the other foot

and thus no longer is it yon bad old days
when the masses were so easily infected by the red malaise
and our class stared up blind cul-de-sacs and alleyways

of course you may happen to witness the occasional binge
which actually helps to cover up an infectious cringe

BALANCING

that ensures a continuation of our region's bland
incompetence
so ignore all those cries of bourgeois decadence

likewise also with our new jerusalems of pretty damp slums
where the tone's been dreadfully lowered by work-shy
bums
who just can't relate to the schemes of our social planners
thus the appalling absence of proper deference and manners

but observe all that sadly underdeveloped real estate space
so neglected by our own unimaginative entrepreneurs
it really is a terrible business and disgrace

so for big-time whizz-kids like yourselves don't
misunderstand
it could prove a real goldmine our dear and friendly land
as it's all up for grabs forest moors and mountains the lot
and it would be a shame to see it all go to pot

and of course don't worry as it'll soon be only a memory
the country's best-forgotten nasty and strife-ridden history
and anyway before long who knows they could all be tory
and then it would all be another story

one of true-blue loyalty trust and glory

Sotto Voce

The last missile
went out in style
but the smell
lingered on
for an awful
long while

The nuclear threat
may
be out of date
But cruelty and hate
continue
as always

The consensus
being
that it was
now all without purpose
we then brought
the sad little lot
to an early close

Too many
had worshipped money
and as a result
were so easily bought

No comment
but plenty
mementoes

How it goes

War Is Murder

Don't be alarmed
Don't be afraid
It's only another futile
Air-raid
Came the muffled statement
From the barricaded basement

But when will the war be over?
Harsh is that sinister cough
Of the murderous mortar

They sent in the tanks
They sent in the planes
They ironed out the kinks
And frazzled our brains
Fear fills the very atmosphere
The city lies in ruins
Craters are everywhere

Repent, repent
It says in the old testament
Some prophet of profit
No doubt

And oh that peristent stink
Of dead bodies, shit and piss

Let's construct and not destruct
Let's call a halt to this
At once
For we are sick of it

> The new world
> order
> is based on
> profit
> torture
> & murder
> therefore
> in no time at all
> it should surely
> win us over
> to a peaceful
> and prosperous
> future
> in which
> we'll all
> live happily
> ever after
> without any fear
> of the time
> to come
>
> Or?

Untitled

So girls,
always point your tips straight
downhill.

Tips?

Aye, tips;
and then control those skis
by symmetrical unweighting
and use of the knees
and we'll all sail
down that steep hill
like
some fleet-of-foot flotilla
of shapely racing-ships
coasting
before the wind.

Ski-ing can be fun
under a low
winter sun.

Untitled

Obviously
one can hasten
one's own
execution
like
Yeltsin
ordering
genocide
on the tiny
Chechen nation
Democratisation
by liquidation?
Now there's a
democratic
propostition
coming from
a new man
and a Russian one
at that

Into the bargain

Men and women
Have one thing in common
Lost children
They all are
In what could have been
A truly humane
Garden of Eden

No Ant Is Trident

How important Trident has become to
us.

And of course we can't
afford an accident
even when the war seems imminent
as the loss
of life
could be enormous,
an odd million or so
if you include
the entire lowlands
as well as greater Glasgow.

Think of a figure
on into infinity
and reflect that the few
who would remain
would at least be healthy,
wealthy and free.

To contemplate it is awful
but nevertheless
think about it.

Trident is vital.

Without it we'd be lost.

Yes,
there is life after death;

of a kind.
And light.
Permanent light.
And smell.
Guilt is inbuilt.
No purpose, no meaning, no fight.
It's inevitable.
People only appear to be people.
All communication is forbidden.
The big black pit is wide and deep
and no one can sleep.
Life is hell.

Untitled

The prisoner
who'd committed murder
gasped for air
when they sat him down
in the electric chair.

No room for manoeuvre.

But soon it was all over,
the death-certificate
was signed
and no one any longer
seemed to mind
that yet another killer
was gone.

Fly Man

Even though you're an anarchist
you always tug your forelock
when the boss goes past.

No harm done after all
as you're not really servile
but a realist.

Phoney Stare

The latest labour-leader,
Phoney Stare
sat contentedly in his
don't-rock-the-boat rocking-chair
clutching a big fat cat
or was it a teddy-bear?

What? A lot of hot air? Me?
Me the great progressive progenitor?
Never, for I wish as always for
us all to be free. Likewise I'm
no ventriloquist but a true
socialist,
even if I did stick my big
grubby paws
all over our sacred clause four.
So please let me be
and let me love my teddy-bear
and thereafter he
sized us all up again with his
fixed phoney stare.

An ant is itinerant

Life is cheap on an antheap
An ant never lifts its eyes to
the horizon
An ant lives on carrion
Ants never seem to sleep
An ant is an assassin
But there's order amidst the
confusion

An ant is almost human

Circle

The mountain sits, sweats and toils
As brown burn water
Like eternal laughter
Boils then falls from the hills
Over moor, wet peat and belled heather

From where the white night-wind whets
its whistling whisper
And spills its cruel chills
Fiercely into the river's meander

A cyclic circle seen by the idle intruder

Without Question

Why did they plant and build so high?
To chain the moon and blot out the sun
and to nail the earth to its afterbirth?
Or to pinion the horizon to an anxious sky,
to blacken all that's human and to shut out death?

Or to reach for a nowhere heaven with no reason
ever given as to why,
when aware of the blind anger that could only
lead to armageddon,
bad were the decisions taken;
conscious also that in the long run the seeds
had been barren.

It was greed that had bled and then buried the ocean.
An accident that was waiting to happen.

Who's got the key?

Who's got the key?
You or me?
Who's got the booze?
Us or youse?
Who's got the phlegm?
Us or them?
But who'll call the shots?
What? Us the Scots?
You must be joking.
Bunch o' robots.
Wi no one tae blame.

Must one know what it's like to grovel and be covered
in spittle in order to stimulate the writing of the
great Scottish novel?

We're passive.
We're conservative.
We withdraw.
We stand in awe.
We walk a tightrope.
We live in hope.
We chatter in a pit.
We champ at the bit.
We'll never get out of it.
We're deep in the shit.

That vital circle
ever
opening
closing
rotating
oscillating
arcing
and without it
the circuit
the centre
is missing
nothing is healed
the source
the secret
with shattering force
must be revealed

Untitled

Did the merry widow
attend the marriage of Figaro?
and if so
was she then put in the shadow?
We'd love to know
here in kulchur-city Glasgow

Betrayed

Latterly
she got laid
in a lovely
forest-glade

But then
for some unknown reason
feeling both dismayed
and betrayed
Goldilocks
scared of HIV, AIDS
and the pox
slew the wolf
or was it a bear?

Then flexing her claws and
taking her spade
she buried him deep
in a wooden box
animal that he was

Gave her a scare

Better
to sing and rage
outside the cage
than be in it
hand-fed
but half-dead
creature of habit
& performing parrot
with some no-go
manifesto

Subterfuge

Something was missing
Terribly
So you took up running
Occasionally
The difference is now amazing
Your whole being scintillating
& reverberating
So is running a cure for everything?
Possibly

Mock-Up

Down come the blinds
when power
is handed over
to the inferior
and mediocre

those with small minds

Scotland is nice
Scotland sells at a bargain price

Scotland is sweet
Scotland is bonnie
Scotland the cheat
Scotland needs money

Scotland the brave
Scotland in fame
Scotland's an open grave
Scotland so tame

Scotland so scenic
Scotland so bland
Scotland is sick
But do try to understand
That cringing tartan mind

BALANCING

They built it
bit by bit
merchants
miscreants
& lumpen proletariat

a city of concrete
with built-in defeat

banners and rebels were hung
answers were too neat

they sang the wrong song
and now it's not theirs
to inherit

not liberty and fraternity
but property and paternity

they deal
with all that's fragile
in the soulless city

Never Again

Barely heard. From behind closed doors
Tongues twitter. Sharp knives clatter.
It is night. Fierce red light shifts.
Through a cluttered sky as stars
Flare beyond our sight. We're blind.

Those sensuous fingers can't be yours
But the past's, which lingers. Let's
Listen for that broken music of the
People. It is also ours and more so
In coming momentuous hours. Cherish
That harmony that once was. But now
It is almost no more. It dies. A cripple.

Peristent echoes are still heard. Minds
Harden. And across the great waste shimmers
A hot horizon. Too many never ever perceive
Or even hear the thistle rustle. Our love
May surface again. And yours too. Just whistle.

Dust clears. Dark laments rise and fill our
Ears. Yes, we hear, we hear the airs. Each
Note addresses those who would kill. Crash
Of sounds, orchestra of revenge and hate
As minds no longer wander. For we remember.
We knew, and say never again. No, never again.

Six Days That Shook You Up
(from *Vechera Rostov*)

Rostov in May 1991

Notes from above ground with the general picture still far
from being clear, as is the near future, something like 30
billions bucks a year seemingly required from Western Aid?

Soviet land so dear to every toiler, soon, the rouble-trouble
getting worse by the minute. Big capital to the rescue of the
perpetual queue, and hopefully also to the Soviet toilet.
These are the facts. Or are they? I mean, who's kidding
who? For there's no need for you to stand, as yet, in any
queue.
Around 150 Glaswegians drawn from all sections of the
community and with all sorts of opinions, preconceived and
otherwise, on the Soviet Union of ex-socialist republics.
Business-men, muscle-men, councillors, actors, singers,
dancers, pipers, painters, tourists and poets. You name it,
they're here, experts to a man - and woman.
How to explain and where to begin? Begin to explain the
passion, contempt, confusion and emotion? To understand
the impressions left - and right, in every mind? You can't as
you suspect more are ignorant than intelligent when it
comes to giving a balanced opinion on this massive
collective called the Soviet Union. Not even yourself as a

lifelong student of it and its glorious proletariat, your first
visit being as a know-all and radical teenager way back
which came as a culture shock, especially when taken to a
poetry-event at the Moscow Dynamo stadium with
probably well over twenty thousand of an audience in
attendance. Astonishing. Seeds were planted and in many
ways we still sang, "Yes Stalin still loves us as the Worker
tells us so."

> "Shower man with all earthly blessings, plunge
> him so deep into happiness that nothing is visible
> but the bubbles rising to the surface of his
> happiness, as if it were water; give him such
> economic prosperity that he will have nothing left
> to do but sleep, eat gingerbread, and worry about
> the continuance of world history - and he, I mean
> man, even then, out of mere ingratitude, out of
> sheer devilment will commit some abomination.
> He will jeopardize his very gingerbread and
> deliberately will the most pernicious rubbish, the
> most uneconomic nonsense, simply and solely in
> order to alloy all this positive rationality with the
> element of his own pernicious fancy."
>
> Fyodor Dostoevsky

The Russian faces on the jam-packed trolley-buses. All
kinds, stoical, many beautiful, wondering what's going on
in their minds. Those who have some room to move their
hands, pass you their tickets for you to punch on the
punch-machine, but your embarrassed interpreters do it for
you. "But oh, how to make your way to the door,
Fyodor!" For it's time, time, punishment without the
crime.
We're so impatient and anxious in the West. They don't

seem to be, they seem to be more at peace with themselves and have a different sense of time, of their place in space. Asiatic perhaps? No, surely not, as they pride themselves in being European. But in any case to me it's a big difference, one I enjoy, as I don't want them to be "exactly" the same as us.

Then there's the humour. Most I met love to laugh, and yes, even at my own sick jokes, for humour's a funny thing, I tell them, and they agree. Very funny. Once I was poor and sick: now I'm healthy, wealthy . . . and tell lies - no I don't, as any poet worth his salt is of course always in pursuit of the truth, even though he's always concentrating on meaning. Death is the only truth there is. Inert and samyert (Russian for death) and no longer so smart.

So quiet flows the Don but not so the monsoon. Bring your summer-togs? Big joke. The weather is quite appalling, especially when it hasn't rained in Glasgow the whole of May. They're blaming it on Kuwait and they could be right, shrinking planet, all of us more or less in the same plight.

> Virgin soil soiled.
> Trouble in Chernobyl.
> Far too many maimed and killed.

A mini-Don runs along the swollen gutter and you hear yourself ask Sophie if she agrees that we're all programmed for disaster.

Can't remember her answer.

Dostoevsky adapted for the theatre.

Astonishing performance by Yuri as he goes through the agonies and occasional delights alone on stage for 1 hour and 45 minutes. The barrier of language though. How long

is the concentration-span of an insane man? Then comes
the most powerful and erotic scene I've ever seen in
theatre. Quite incredible as the crucified Yuri is at long last
in harness with the universe. Or is he? Christ knows.
Then in the vodka-soaked aftermath you go into dialogue
with the actress (can't remember her name) through an
interpreter into the wee small hours about Dostoevsky's
message for the world today. We dug deep, very deep, if I
remember right.

> Becoming something frightening
> as we spun alone and rudderless
> into a nowhere here and there
> lost in dust and without trace
> helpless to share
> in our deep-rooted fear

Hopefully we'll meet again and continue our discussion, all
about the soul and what's good and what's evil, you poseur
of an intellectual, you.
Over breakfast a businessman tells me he visited an
astonishing ball-bearing factory, vast and almost all
automated, and a lecturer tells me the sports-clinic-centre is
out of this world. So it looks as if some of us are impressed,
though others aren't. Others are scathing about the
shortcomings that they see and experience, without really
trying to understand the reasons. Like, for instance, the
reason for the shortage of matches is apparently that the
factory where they're made is much too close to Chernobyl
for comfort, with the result that labout is in extremely short
supply.
Nothing is simple. All is complex. Should always ask why.
Top tables and separate eating-rooms for our creme-de-la-

creme. Them and us. Cabal and the rabble. Distinguished
guests and necessary pests, the Glasgow hoi-polloi.
Comment from an old Russian-lover: "It's this kind of
thing that's caused all the trouble here and elsewhere in the
Soviet empire. Look at Honecker and Ceacescu. Nothing's
new."

> Chants from the past; Polish Free Youth on
> Gydinia docks:
> Stalin! Gottwald! Pieck! Engels and Karl Marx!
> Everywhere the youth are singing freedom's song
> and we unite to show the world that
> we are . . . wrong?

You're staying on the 13th floor of the Intourist Hotel and
from your room you can see for miles way over the Don
and across the steppes. Not a mountain to be seen
anywhere. Flat land. Flat but not yet wide open to the
world. At one time the malaria and cholera must have been
bad. Sholokhov's novels tell it all and you'll need to go
back and read them again.
You hum the song *Stenka Rasin* to yourself, trying to shut-
out the constant roar or the heavy traffic below. How
different it all must have been before the car. Cossacks on
horses and in peace?

Disappointed that not one public reading had been
arranged, nevertheless you absolutely enjoy your readings
and meetings with the so alert students in English at the
Pedagogical Institute. The test is always in the reading and,
no matter that you had to do a "lecture" on "Scottish
Writing Today", the rest went well going by the response
afterwards. Many questions and invitations.
Yes, this indeed is the land of poetry-lovers, but of clarity

and not obscurity. Poems with meaning and singing, like
with Blok, Pasternak, Khlebnikhov and Lermontov, not to
mention Esenin and Pushkin.

My "Once We Had A Dream" . . .
>   The lumpen would live in some seventh heaven
>   And it would be each according to his need
>   In a comradely Eden . . .

is apparently very appropriate to the Russian situation of
today. Publication? We'll see.
Defending the USSR?
Most of your life you've done so no matter the problems,
the frustrations, contradictions and incarcertions seemingly
inherent in what was called the first socialist experiment,
and how you still remember well your extrememly short
spell in the YCL. You radical, you!
State socialism, state capitalism, both programmed for
cataclysm? The argument goes on. How to plan it that our
planet can be exploited for profit. Is this the road forward?
Or backward?
Over meals you find yourself as ever practising you own
brand of dialectic with so many people who know such a
little, and yet they think they know it all. They see what's
real but fail to appreciate all that's spiritual in the Russian
soul, which seems to be not too obsessed with buying and
selling and making a killing, and wondering if this is a good
or a bad thing. No, somehow the dialectic must analyze and
cope with the materialistic otherwise we're doomed, for
our planet is not limitless but finite.
Prostitution and exploitation the end-solution? Never. Is
there a cure for greed and fever?
No, they must not, and probably will not, try to imitate
what's best - and worst, in the West.

BALANCING

That would be fatal. Like down in the cellar, in the hotel-bar, where it's raucous music and ladies for hire.

> "But man is so partial to systems and abstract deductions that in order to justify his logic he is prepared to distort the truth intentionally. Look around you, everywhere blood flows in torrents . . ."
>
> Fyodor Dostoevsky

In a restaurant in Azov a woman who heard you reading presents you with a bottle of precious Stolichnaya vodka. She thought I was great even though my name is Jack and not Peter.
One more member of my fan-club. Soon be in double figures at this rate. Lovely woman.
Soviet toilets so wearing to every foreigner, let's face it, though many of our women can't we hear. Lurid experiences everywhere, when it's not too sweet sitting on the seat - if there is one, that is.
So there you are waiting for a boat and suddenly needing to shit, but where do you do it, you agonised poet? Then the boat appears and your worst fears are justified - there ain't no toilet on it. So concentrate, otherwise it might be too late, even though you're desperate and have no idea where we're heading, out on to the Sea of Azov somewhere. Slow boat to China? Chug-chug-chug goes the old tug-boat. You've told the interpreter of course and soon everyone in the party (no, not the CP) knows it that Jack is dying for a . . . but as luck would have it we discover that we're on the wrong boat as this faster boat with its gesticulating skipper appears from the other direction, passes us, and heads for the same base we've just come from. Cheers all

round. I don't dare. But yes, yes our new boat has a toilet
deep down in the bowels somewhere. No seat but clean.
Who cares? I don't.
End of another hilarious incident and hygenic dialect.
The beggars outside and inside the holy places interest
everyone, especially our cameramen. Burns' Jolly Beggars
don't have a look in with this lot as they hold their
smoking-bowls before them trying to get the wherewithal
to build that New Jerusalem.

> A fig for those by law protected
> Liberty's a glorious feast
> Courts for cowards were erected
> Churches built to please the priest
>
> Robert Burns

Religion a panacea for consumption and perpetual
revolution in the spiritual hole of Holy Russia? If so, then
perhaps indeed Alexander Solzhenitsyn has the solution,
another kind of song but still all wrong? A harvest with
interest down on the Don?

> A real Russian doll but on call, this was as obvious
> as the nose on one's face.
> Forget about Lenin and con them with Mammon?
> Have you satisfied your hunger with the new
> market commodity?
> Now that magic has lost its power over you?
> Marina Tsvetaeva

To me, after a long analysis, these people are anarchistic to
the core, therefore, surely centralized planning was the
wrong option chosen.

BALANCING

Stalin claimed that communism fitted the Germans like a
saddle fits a cow. What then about his own form of
"communism"? Was it an alien system he tried to impose
on them? Maybe they should examine Kropotkin,
Proudhon, Paine and Bakunin again, though it's always a
very dubious "maybe" when trying to determine what we
mean by "free".

> "But here, on Russian soil, there are no fools, as
> everybody knows: that is what distinguishes us
> from all the other, Germanic countries.
> Consequently, transcendental souls are not found
> among us in their pure form . . . We don't know
> ourselves. And it would be worse for us if our
> stupid whims were indulged. Just try giving us, for
> example, as much independence as possible, untie
> the hands of any one of us, loosen our bonds, and
> we . . . I assure you we should all immediately beg
> to go back under discipline . . ."
>
> Fyodor Dostoevsky

You love their humaneness and seemingly instinctive and
open response and you hope they never become, or try to
become, Western sophisticated and thus false.
Thought: is it innate or has it come about by benevolent
experiment through distant diktat from an understanding
state?
Much closer together and therefore more trust in each
other. This is obvious. This is the near future. Or?
But no more magic dialect? Everything static with no
dynamic, the old ideals murdered by con-men and broad-
church fools.
What do you think of Rostov? What an impossible question

as you can't claim to know Glasgow never mind Rostov.
But like in your own city you see certain signs of social
deprivation and poverty. You see holes in the road and
people worshipping god. You see men on the booze and
semi-static queues. You see many fine buildings in a sorry
state of disrepair but then remember the terrible devastation
in their Great Patriotic War. You see the lovely children
play and chatter, those little ones who must learn from the
past if they're to have any sane and peaceful future.

> Order everywhere, and cleanness,
> Not a fag-end in sight,
> Afraid and unthinking, the soldier sighed
> "This is culture all right."
>
> Aleksander Tvardovsky

A bit like a tourist visiting Glasgow, Joe, the piper, got
stung by a cossack mosquito. Better that than the Trotskys?
Me? I can't go. Not vegetable trouble but the diet of
vodka, kasha and meat, unable to shoot down all the yes-
men united on the toilet-seat, internal systems choking-up
and grinding to a halt. It's all so difficult.
I mean, are the pressing problems of each other's
government, establishment and environment all that
different? For any real analysis surely must recognise that all
socialist and capitalist economies are founded on a
fundamentally dangerous-for-the-entire-species basis, a case
of chaos and crisis. So should the West invest in Glasnost or
not in the attempt to stop the rot and keep a wasteful
Moloch afloat?

> "Capitalism can be utterly vanquished, and will be
> utterly vanquished, by the fact that Socialism

creates a new and much higher productivity of
labour. This is a very difficult matter and must
take considerable time . . ."

V I Lenin

One can't experiment with a sleeping giant even when the
time seems urgent.
You'd say Rostov is cleaner, less litter, but maybe Glasgow
is greener. Maybe, as no maps were handed out, the
Russians still seemingly obsessed by keeping many things
secret.

> North south east & west
> No sense of direction
> Nowhere to rest

Song and poetry exchange with Yuri and Fiona, the actors,
the vodka flowing faster than the Don.
He takes you by the shoulders and delivers sweet
Khlebnikov music straight into your eyes. You answer with
Burns and one of you own. No surprise. And so it goes on,
the whole night through close to the dawn, and it was real
good, no language barrier. We all understood.
But the sky is so dark and sadly not red.
After the fall of the wall is socialism as vision and goal no
longer viable in the Russian soul? And if so, what's going to
fill the vacuum and hole? A so-called free market for the
proletariat which fluctuating from slump to boom must
inevitably end in universal doom and collapse into chaos?
No more dreams of transformation through imagination and
progressive revolution with only a sick semblance of
transnational capital spirals out of control, not so trivial,
banal and bloody lethal?

Think about it carefully, you mighty Russian people.
With the weather everywhere becoming an everyday
nightmare.
Not to forget that the individual if he or she wants to be
whole must become a social animal and not yield to that
need for greed and urge for speed. But freedom of
movement is vitally important as frontiers become more and
more permanent. If people are able to travel then they're
more likely to settle and not rebel against their own little
local hell. Then and only then, perhaps, can freedom from
serfdom become freedom from boredom, which all of us
suffer from having lived for so long under threat from the
bomb.
So, back in Glasgow, I think of Rostov and send it my
love.
How I yearn to return.

Sequence Dance

Yet
again you reiterate
that man's fate
is not to sit
back and let himself
be dominated
by the endless edicts
of system and state
but to look
learn
deliver and love
and liberate

Semi-circular step sequence
Done with such insouciance
So shall we dance?
It's in your nature
To be a failure
Without any future
Because your self-taught?
So what
At least you can't be bought
And become a puerile puppet
Or robot
And who is it anyway
Who's out of kilter with nature?
Not this shrewd Scot
As he's a real thinker
I'd do you a shiatsu
If only I knew how to

But hopefully you will continue
To do me a shiatsu
As each time that you do
I feel as if I'm born anew
And feel like a baby
On the bottle
With eyes of azure blue

There's always
something missing
in package-holidays
swimming
snorkelling
sand and sun
are fun
but then the eyes soon
begin to glaze

Who are we
to disagree
Who are we
when no longer free
units
idiots
robots
and all at sea

You'd kill the cunt
as soon as look at him
or even at a whim
So best to keep well distant
and suppress your odium
Don't want

to end up behind bars
cut-off from the stars
faced with a conviction
and conundrum
and counting out time
for killing is a crime

Don't slumber
Adenauer
Every time
For remember
Eisenhower
And his claim
And climb
To power
Big dig for victory
Think of Hitler
Then go and have a shower

Untitled

They found a fossil all stony
In Possil
That looked like a thistle
But they sold it
Of course for a song & a whistle
As they desperately
Needed the money

Light

It had been a long time. Things were seemingly again normal. I walked rather unsteadily across the vast field towards the beckoning sunset. The air still shimmered with the fading heat of the day. I began to sweat. And the insects were out, my face their feeding-ground. All was so still. Except for the usual sounds. The sky was now like blood. Earth merging with heaven and ocean. Balanced. On the edge. My feet sounded hollow below. On and on. And on. Ceaseless. With no prospects of ever stopping. The thought made me shudder and tremble. Quake as well as sweat. The horizon wavered. Things were no longer so normal. As seemed. I could not bear it. It was too much for me. I let go. Had to let go. And then in the fall heard myself scream. A thing of its own. On and on. And on. Dying to a sob. Good though that I was alone. No, not so good. But at least thankful of the solitude. For the solitude. And yet not. This was perhaps the cause of the disturbance. And the effect. Perhaps. Then it fell across me. A shadow. I froze. Dead in my tracks. It was not mine. Could not possible be mine. The sun was by now well down. Darkness was creeping in. The urge came upon me to scream again. But I was unable to. My tongue was dry and huge. I shut my eyes tight for what seemed like an eternity. Slowly opened them. No escape. It was still there ahead of me. I was somehow forced to turn and face the substance of the thing. Its essence. My heart sounded in my ears like a drum. It was without shape. Enormous. Hideous but beautiful. Eyeless. I was appalled. Overwhelmed. Then it struck me. With the force of a thunderbolt. Smashed to the ground. Pulp. In fragments. All open again to the light. Eternal light. Straight from the centre. Jesus Christ. Oh my God. Help.

No Return

Only eternal night
No more day
No more light
Onwards our flight
On its mindless endless way
Atoms alone in this
Universal time-bomb
We race through space
Hurtle
In a fast relentless stream
Within an open circle

    Vast the distance now
    From our one-time home
    Star to quasar
    Our trajectory is not direct
    But circular
    On a great sweeping ring
    Curved
    Like a trambling cello-string
    Reverberating
    Bending without meaning
    When once we had
    Lived and loved
    Remember that solo singing

Absurd
With no apparent reward
The existence
And functional tasks
Of our dwindling team
The avant-garde
Of the silent scream
Aware of the risks
Blind in a vacuum
Like pawns
In some higher crazy game
Illusions and visions
Failing to bridge the aeons

Aye and now how we drift
Senseless and soft
Across the ether
Withdrawn each soul and brain
From each the other
Amidst the unnerving silence
And continuous indifference
Shielding all that's within
Moving and disturbing
In the finite womb
Feelings smouldering
But never bursting
Into flame
Unable ever to forget
Our remit and set target
And understandably that
Remote blue planet
We once called home

BALANCING

Missionless and without a tryst
We sail on to a non-horizon
Through a limitless mist
Of detritus and stellar dust
There can be no destination
For there is no escape
From this featureless landscape
No yggdrasil or coming zion
The age-old religious question

       But we continue
       We have to
       Like remainders and reminders
       Of that obscene and open human zoo
       Craven strangers and creatures
       Now only a few
       Who seen in a mirror
       Now know that their brief adventure
       Ensures no future in nature
       A picture of terror but true

It's been centuries
Those years not light but dark and quick
Our moving boring but erratic
Still so small and ill
Unable to handle the verities
Absolutes and universal mysteries

       Space has no visible surface
       Its essence of shapelessness
       Coming to us as being full of menace
       Thus our continuous fear and stress
       All reflections and suppositions

Reaching as always
An inevitable impasse
It all seems so pointless

And yet we go on
Like some drifting withdrawn swan
On the retreat
Dying on our feet
Seeking another life-giving sun
Never accepting defeat
Even when we're broken and undone
An energy-arc on a dark horizon
The lightning frightening
A spiralling trail in vision

Here is nowhere
There is anywhere
Enclosed in a chrysalis of fear
We hang songless and soulless
Like a bitsy bauble on a string
Purposeless and useless

Somewhere up beyond
And out of mind
Must come an end
In transit and orbit
All that we were smashed through sound
Into oblivion
We await it with apprehension
Irrational and blind

Cloud on the Clyde

You went tae work as usual
The journey as ever better than the arrival.

The tram was fu' o men in dongarees
Their piece boxes stacked wi chits and cheese.

It wis aa the way tae Govan and then back again;
O tae hae been a shepherd and no an electrician.

Everybody wis smokin, though few were talkin,
Maist coughin and splutterin as if they were chokin.

Then jist afore 8 it wis through the huge gate
As yir wages were cut if ye turned up late.

Straight ower tae the dock, nae time tae pause,
Then bingo all of a sudden the riveters cut loose.

Christ whit a sound not at all profound tore at the air;
Why it couldnae have been ony worse during the 2nd
World War.

So it wis get stuck in there the best ye cin dae
Beastin away guid style till the end o the day.

Some team they were, whit an amazing crowd,
Yon army o fine men who built the great ships o the Clyde.

Samizdat

Tension
    can often be quite acute in an institute particularly
    when you get an insolent dissident in the establishment
        No surprise
        for maybe it's like a baby
        who never cries
        and sanitary worry multiplies

Achtung
pardon
none
hold your tongue
swallows sweet in each institution
    where few can refute murderous memories of a grimm
    jack
    boot as hansel or gretel write another zettel but
        . . . fortunately no longer
        crawl kill or shoot despite
        each slight curdled with
        spite on top of that persistent kleinigkeit

So
light light
let there be
more light
as big G purportedly said
on his deathbed

BALANCING

no doubt aware that might remains mute but significant
under the weight of all that richtigkeit and so-called
no congealed and so cold but real scary freiheit
with most exits closed
but still more questions
to be posed like what's it to be

Arbeit macht light
odour
night
scared to ask why
manipulated then liquidated and in the end faultless
but frei
biting on the bullet and waiting for the pale pink ink
to dry

Remember Pearl Harbour

As reluctant killer you've watched many a fly, bluebottle, cockroach and spider die as you splattered them up against either wall or window with one solid rolled-up newspaper. And sure what a filthy mess it is to be cleaned up later. Has to be done though, for no human home can tolerate such unwelcome guests, pests and intruders. Yes, everywhere are murderers, like, for instance, when your cat caught a big fat rat once, teasing it, toying with it, then finally killing it. Horror. And all you could do was stand and stare and being made aware that there was no escaping death, hidden, sudden or whatever, such is nature, the precarious path through it being such a risky venture with never a hint or glimpse of what or may not come after. No destination but total elimination with not a chance of reincarnation. Or? And then there is no answer or logical reason as to why the enormous slaughter in the second world war. But you seek one as to why the invention of the gun and why man seems destined for self-destruction. This is why you regularly watch "The World at War" on TV in order to see the all-too-real appalling evidence, menace and madness of human existence. Progress? Caring, sharing, loving, understanding? No chance. As I thump yet another bluebottle and shut my ears to its alien death-rattle.

Kilted

Clothed
you descended from the hill
swiftly but cold

Scarred
you shared with but scorned
the sheep in the fold

Battle-hardened
you fought and thought
with quick hand
and honed mind

Naked you'll slide without sound over moor and through
forest
stunned by the wind

And then you'll be gone
broken and blind

Check

Check
Cheque-card
pay-slip cheque-book
key-card house-keys
library-card
work master-key
loose cash
various notes
miscellaneous trash

remember your number

no hash
once-bitten most often
forgotten
with interest

a regulated ribbon
to tie-up tightly
to that expanding horizon
of more illusion
and hallucination

progress is stress